God's

Riddle

The Subtleties of Eternity

Eternity Volume 3

Joseph Kahuho Gatoto

God's Riddle - The Subtleties of Eternity   Joseph Kahuho Gatoto

God's Riddle - The Subtleties of Eternity

Eternity Volume 3

Author Contacts

Phone +254715656938 (WhatsApp and Calls)

Email: intergratedlifeministry@gmail.com

Facebook: Kahuho Gatoto

YouTube: Kahuho Gatoto

Feel free to contact me for questions, comments, seminars, and other ministry invitations.

God's Riddle - The Subtleties of Eternity   Joseph Kahuho
Gatoto

The Integrated School

The Integrated School (School of Mysticism and Metaphysics) is available on "the teachable" online platform. There resides a series of lectures not projected on YouTube. Please feel free to join our online course for exclusive content.

Link:https://integrated-life-ministry-s-school.teachable.com

Contact us through the following numbers for more information or to partner with us:

Pst. Brain 0715349940
Pst. Joseph 0715656938

Books in the ongoing Reality Series

Reality Volume 1

God's Riddle - The Subtleties of Eternity   Joseph Kahuho Gatoto

<u>Reality Series Volume 2 (On Going)</u>

1. The Book of Consciousness and Electromagnetism - The Electromagnetics of Consciousness and Creation

2. The Book of Consciousness and Electromagnetism - The Electromagnetics of Consciousness and Creation Volume 2

3. The Riddle of God: The Subtleties of Eternity - Eternity Volume 3

4. The Book of Consciousness and Electromagnetism - The Electromagnetics of Consciousness and Creation Volume 3: Realms of Origin, Astrology, and Astronomy (TBR)

5. God is Dead, The Truth on Death, the Tree of Life, The Tree of Knowledge of Good and Evil, With the Realms of Eternity, and The Realm of Eternity – Eternity Volume 4 (TBR)

6. Talks With Wisdom – Eternity Volume 5

Available on amazon.com and its affiliates

Remarks on The Reality Series

Isn't it just so great when you find one of those books that completely drags you in, makes you fall in love with God and demands that you sit on the edge of your seat to discover the unknown? This (Book 19: Ecstasy: The Truth Concerning Pleasure and Happiness) is one of those books. Looking forward to reading it – more slowly and spending more time on the details of Pleasure.

Dinah Wanjiku

Reader in Nairobi Kenya

This book on oneness (book 16) is a heavenly Portal and not just a mere book like any other; it is. according to my language, a living epistle bearing the Spirit of the letter, that which quickens. You cannot be a Kingdom mystic in Christ and ignore this book. I am a living witness to what I have experienced and continue to experience Supernaturally through the Heavenly Portal of this book. I recommend that You Consider a Multi-dimensional journey of Supernatural experience by reading & analytically studying this book through the lens of the Spirit.

Apostle Joe Kennedy (Voice of Thunders)

God's Riddle - The Subtleties of Eternity   Joseph Kahuho Gatoto

House Of Thunders International

Mombasa, Kenya

I recommend this great curriculum to the Body of Christ all over the world, especially those who want to walk in the present-day manifestation of the sons of God. Every book is a sequence of the other. You cannot understand book 2 if you have not read book 1. I recommend if you are getting these books to get book 1.

Prophet Samuel Njagi

School of Supernatural Empowerment International

Kenya

This book (Book 7: Reality of Music) will stretch your understanding and implications of music in you as a becoming individual by helping you understand what music is, how music precedes man, and how every human has a propensity towards music.

Gift Isezerano

Reader in Nairobi, Kenya

God's Riddle - The Subtleties of Eternity   Joseph Kahuho
Gatoto

I would recommend the book (7) to everyone who is musical
and has been called to serve in the music ministry. It has deep
insights unveiled to the world.

Mary Patricia Nyaboke

Librarian at Gospel Garden Bible School

Dedication

To

Those that desire to know Him more and to know His hiding place and places.

Introduction

"To understand a proverb and an enigma,
The words of the wise and their riddles." Proverbs 1:6
NKJV

An original poem for the glory of the King:

Wisdom teaches Her ways,

By concealing Her Beauty in understanding;

Employing Her might in the counsel of Her knowledge:

That man may seek Her in Her Darkness -

In those Her dark sayings that cover Her Holy Nakedness -

Her Omnipotent Light that covers Her Nakedness:

The Spirit that She is, the Mighty LORD and God;

The Subtle One in all Her subtleties!

- Joseph Kahuho Gatoto

For more poems akin to this read ***Incongruent Congruents - Poems of Formation in Reality Series Volume 1***.

"*It is* the glory of God to conceal a matter,

But the glory of kings *is* to search out a matter." Proverbs 25:2 NKJV

"Give ear, O my people, *to* my law;

Incline your ears to the words of my mouth.

I will open my mouth in a parable;

I will utter dark sayings of old,

Which we have heard and known,

And our fathers have told us.

We will not hide *them* from their children,

Telling to the generation to come the praises of the Lord,

And His strength and His wonderful works that He has done." Psalm 78:1-4NKJV

"If a man desire much experience, she *(wisdom)* knoweth things of old, and conjectureth aright what is to come: she knoweth the subtilties of speeches, and can expound dark sentences: she foreseeth signs and wonders, and the events of seasons and times." Wisdom of Solomon 8:8 KJV

"The wise man will seek out the wisdom of all the ancients and will be occupied in the prophets. He will keep the sayings of renowned men and will enter withal into the subtleties of parables. He will search out the hidden meanings of proverbs, and will be conversant in the secrets of parables." Ecclesiasticus 39:1-3 KJV

Chapter 1

The Hidden One

"He made darkness His secret place;

His canopy around Him was dark waters

And thick clouds of the skies." Psalm 18:11 NKJV

And I stood with the Holy One, before the Holy One in a vision while in meditation. There we stood before His Darkness, Himself; and there into Himself He took me through Darkness to His Light, Himself, in the Darkness, Himself. Eternity is hidden in Himself, in the Darkness that is Him, and revealed from Himself being hidden in Himself. He is hidden yet revealed. In His revelation of Himself, He hides. The Self He reveals, Himself, is hidden in Himself. He is the Subtle One. The Seen and Unseen. The Seer that sees all and knows all; yet is unseen by all though seen in all, for all things, all forms, are shadows of His Formless Form, Himself. He is the Substance of all things, which are shadows of Him from Him. Hiddenness is His nature, His essence and the structure from which all things hide in themselves and reveal themselves from themselves.

Volume 1

The Subtleties of Eternity

"..she knoweth the subtleties of speeches..." The Wisdom of Solomon 8:8 KJV

He says: "Son of man, pose a riddle, and speak a parable to the house of Israel..." Ezekiel 17:2 NKJV. Again, He says: "Inasmuch as an excellent spirit, knowledge, understanding, interpreting dreams, solving riddles, and explaining enigmas were found in this Daniel, whom the king named Belteshazzar, now let Daniel be called, and he will give the interpretation." Daniel 5:12 NKJV. By what means were the aforementioned found in Daniel? It is written: "As for these four young men (Daniel, Shadrach, Meshach, and Abednego), God gave them knowledge and skill in all literature and wisdom; and Daniel had understanding in all visions and dreams." Daniel 1:17 NKJV. When it said God gave them knowledge, skill which is understanding and wisdom in knowledge, and wisdom, with understanding in all visions and all visions and dreams to Daniel, it meant the Spirit of Knowledge, Wisdom, and Understanding. Still, did they not demonstrate the fear of the Lord by choosing not to defile themselves? The Spirit of the Fear of the Lord; of which it is written: "The fear of the LORD is the beginning of knowledge, But fools despise wisdom and instruction." Proverbs 1:7 NKJV. The fear of the Lord is by the Spirit of the Lord, Which is the beginning of knowledge, that is the beginning of the Spirit of Knowledge; the beginning of accessing the Spirit of Knowledge. And in this instance: of accessing the knowledge of the subtleties of Eternity. Now, where there is knowledge, there is understanding, and wisdom and might in knowledge in wisdom. Aren't the wise mighty in wisdom? Are not the knowledgeable mighty in their knowledge and from the same? Those with knowledge do not perish because of the might in knowledge which is the Spirit of Might (Hosea 4:6). Those with understanding are mighty in their understanding and from their understanding. Further, these are revered for their counsel which they attain in their knowledge, wisdom, understanding, and might.

Enigmas, Riddles, and Proverbs

"To understand a proverb and an enigma, The words of the wise and their riddles." Proverbs 1:6 NKJV

What is a proverb? What is a riddle? What is an enigma? It is knowledge that has been understood and concealed in wisdom by understanding. Words of understanding are hidden in knowledge by the wisdom of understanding in understanding. And what are riddles? Words of the wise, wisdom, concealed in knowledge through understanding. What are enigmas? The problems of the wise; articulated in their knowledge of wisdom in the understanding of their wisdom. By understanding a proverb, a riddle, and an enigma, a man of understanding attains wise counsel through the wisdom in their understanding and the wisdom in their understanding. By grasping the same a wise man increases in learning in the understanding of their wisdom and from the same. In understanding the same, a man of understanding increases in knowledge and becomes wise in the wisdom of their knowledge, attaining understanding in their understanding. Still, in knowing, and understanding the same a man that fears the Lord comes to knowledge and knows wisdom in the understanding of knowledge from the fear of the Lord and in the fear of the Lord. Didn't Israel marvel at the wisdom of King Solomon which was demonstrated by the Spirit of Wisdom in the understanding of the knowledge of the incident between the two prostitutes? Wasn't the solution a counsel from wisdom? From the counsel of wisdom in wisdom by the understanding of wisdom in the knowledge of wisdom? And what was this marvelling? It was reverence, awe, a tremendous fear from the Spirit of the Fear of the Lord in the Spirit of Wisdom. Men fear, and revere, the wise in their wisdom in the understanding of their wisdom and the knowledge in their wisdom that displays the might of wisdom in their knowledge and counsel.

"And all Israel heard of the judgment which the king had rendered; and they feared the king, for they saw that the wisdom of God was in him to administer justice." 1 Kings 3:28 NKJV

The Spirit of Understanding

"The Spirit of understanding…" Isaiah 11:2 NKJV

The Spirit of Understanding conceals Himself in words of understanding from the counsel of understanding that understands counsel and attains the same in understanding counsel from its understanding; concealing understanding in understanding. In understanding, understanding conceals itself with understanding that the man of understanding may understand in understanding with understanding from their understanding, thereby understanding understanding. It takes understanding to understand understanding, and it takes understanding to reveal hidden understanding. What is understood is hidden from being understood because it is understood, and this is done by understanding with the might of understanding which understands the might of understanding. Understanding possesses words of understanding that hide understanding for the understanding that seeks out understanding to understand. The Spirit of Understanding is hidden in Himself by the might of understanding in the wisdom of understanding, and in the knowledge of understanding with the wisdom of knowledge.

The aforementioned are Spirits in the Spirit of Understanding and are the Spirit of Understanding Which is God, Eternity Himself.

Volume 1.3

The Spirit of Wisdom

"The Spirit of wisdom…" Isaiah 11:2 NKJV

The Spirit of Wisdom hides in Herself and in Himself with words of wisdom, the words of the wise from the counsel of wisdom in the wisdom of counsel which possess counsel. Keeping Himself and Herself for the wise that seek wisdom in wisdom by wisdom. It takes wisdom to get wisdom, and wisdom to get to wisdom in wisdom. Wisdom knows Her hiding place. Wisdom knows where He hides and only She can take men there. Still, in the understanding of wisdom does wisdom hide, in the same understanding does wisdom reveal Herself from Himself. By the knowledge of wisdom does wisdom hide, by the same does She manifest Himself using the tools of Her hiding: the words of the wise which are the knowledge of wisdom in the understanding of wisdom. The same demonstrates the might of wisdom through which wisdom hides in the knowledge of Her wisdom, and in understanding of His wisdom with the might of the understanding of might. The aforementioned are Spirits in the Spirit of Wisdom and are the Spirit of Wisdom that is God.

Volume 1.4

The Spirit of Might

"The Spirit of might…" Isaiah 11:2 NKJV

In the understanding of might does the Spirit of Might reveal might; by might the Spirit hides in Its might having command of Its power in the knowledge of power by the understanding of power with the wisdom of power in the counsel of power that counsels power by the council of power. By these, Its knowledge, wisdom, and understanding of might, does the Spirit hide Itself by Its counsel in the wisdom of might and the understanding of might in the knowledge of might and by the council of might. What are the aforementioned but Spirits in the Spirit of Might Which are the Same Spirit Which is God.

The Spirit of Counsel

"The Spirit of counsel…" Isaiah 11:2 NKJV

By the council of the Spirit of Counsel does counsel hide in counsel by and in understanding Itself from Itself by Itself, Its own council; comprised of the understanding of council and counsel, the knowledge of council and counsel, the power of counsel and council, with the wisdom of counsel and council. Still, by the wisdom of counsel and the counsel in the council of the Spirit of Counsel does the Same conceal and reveal Himself from Himself. And what are the aforementioned but Spirits in the Spirit of Counsel that are the Same Spirit that is God.

Volume 1.6

The Spirit of Knowledge

"The Spirit of knowledge…" Isaiah 11:2 NKJV

Knowledge hides knowledge in knowledge in understanding of knowledge, in the wisdom of knowledge, in the counsel of knowledge from the council of knowledge, with the might of knowledge and by the same reveals itself from itself. And what are these, the aforementioned, but Spirits in the Spirit of Knowledge that are the Same Spirit Who is God.

Chapter 2

Samson's Riddle

"Out of the eater came something to eat, And out of the strong came something sweet." Judges 14:14 (NKJV)

By the knowledge of might, in the understanding of might, with the counsel of might, in the wisdom of might, and fear of might in the aforementioned, Samson concealed might using might and revealed might using might by words of the wise and words of understanding through which he hid knowledge and revealed knowledge in the understanding of knowledge with the wisdom of knowledge, and by the counsel of wisdom, knowledge, and understanding.

Volume 1

Out of the eater

"Out of the eater came something to eat, And out of the strong came something sweet." Judges 14:14 NKJV

Out of means from the inner structure and chambers of the eater. Now, that which is out of is in the nature of and is as that which it has come out of. It may be of a different form, taste, and scent but it is not different from its origin. It is one with its origin. Its interiors are the interiors of its origin. It is the origin made manifest within its structure. So, what came from the eater is food because what the eater ate is food. Food from food. Again, food goes within and becomes the body of the eater, which is the eater. You are your body and your body is you. Ergo, out of the eater also means out from the body of the eater which is the eater. And this, the body, is from the interiors of the eater and is one dimension of the eater which also becomes part and parcel of the interiors of the eater. You are what you eat. You become what you eat. From what the eater ate, came what the eater became. Food came from food. Food comes from food. As it is written: "each producing fruit according to its kind." Again, "...these I have given you for food." And where did these, foods, come from? From the Earth! Earth is the food of man. All the foods of man are Earth. Man is of Earth and eats what is of Earth, that came from the interiors of the Earth from the interiors of Eternity. Eternity is the food of man! As it is written: "Man shall not live by bread alone but by every word that comes out of the mouth of the Lord." The bread is food from the Earth which is food from Eternity Himself which came by the word, His word, Himself, when He said: "Let the Earth produce trees with fruits and seeds according to their kind...and herbs of all kind." Man shall not live by these alone but by every word that comes out of the mouth of the Lord. Out of the abundance of the heart, the mouth speaks. That is, out of the interiors of the self, the self speaks; out of the inner realities of the Lord, the Lord speaks. The Lord is the Eater and out of Him, Himself, man is to eat. God is the food of man. "Man shall not live by bread alone but by every word." And that word is the Lord: "...unless you eat of my flesh and drink of my word...", Again, "I am the bread that came down from heaven." Still: "the Word became flesh and dwelt amongst us." John 14:6 NKJV. And, "In the beginning was the Word, and the Word was with God, and the Word was God. He was in the beginning with God. All things were made through Him, and without Him nothing was made that was made." John 1:1-3 NKJV

Volume 2

The Eater

The eater, the Lion, devours and consumes. Brings life to an end. The prey cannot be saved from the Lion's hand. As it is written: "Shall the prey be taken from the mighty?" Isaiah 49:24 NKJV. What is it in the Lord that consumes, and brings things to an end? Is it not Omega? The Lion of Judah and the Great Lion are Omega. The end is the eater, the consumer of all things, and this is Omega. There is the Alpha in Omega and the Omega in the Alpha. The end in the beginning and the beginning in the end. That is the End in the Beginning and the Beginning in the End. As it is written: "I am the Alpha and Omega. The First and the Last. The Beginning and the End." There is might in the beginning, the might of beginning, and there is might in the end, the might of ending in the end. The beginning generates beginnings and the end generates endings and these are one. The Eater is the Giver and the Giver is the Eater. The End of Life is the Beginning of Life. So, in the Spirit of Might, there is the Might of Beginnings and the Might of Ends. Might begins in Might and Might ends in Might. Might is its beginning and its end - the Alpha and Omega within its Infinite Multiple Diversities - Itself.

Something to Eat

That which eats is eaten. The consumer is consumed. This is a working of the Great Eater, a manifestation of the Great Eater within the structure of Himself that is Himself; His Consciousness, per the Cosmic Principle of Karma and or Seed and Fruit, which is Himself in manifestation from Himself within the parameters of Himself as Justice. You reap what you sow. The eater produces something to eat because he himself eats. And this product is within the Cosmic Principle of Productivity and Manifestation: Consciousness must manifest, be productive from Itself by Itself and through Itself for Itself. It is in all forms of consciousness to produce. Consciousness is Production Itself. The Intelligence of Production. Still, what Consciousness produces from Itself it produces for Itself as well within the bounds of Itself per Its self-interacting and self-awareness reality. This is: Seed and Fruit, Karma in operation and manifestation, consciousness Itself experiencing Itself. Life is self-experience. It is experiencing the self from the self. Within the operations of self-awareness: what happens to you is you happening to you.

You are a happening that happens to yourself from yourself and in yourself. Something to Eat is fruit from eating. It is you being consumed from what you consumed. What you consume consumes you.

The End in the Beginning and the Beginning in the End

"I am the Beginning and the End" Revelation 1:8 NKJV

First, there was the Eater, and at the End of the Eater came something to Eat from which comes the strength of the Eater once it is eaten and consumed. There is the Beginning at the End of the Beginning and the End of the End from the Beginning of the End. Out of the Eater - The Beginning, came - at the End of the Beginning, Something to Eat, that had a beginning in the End of the Beginning, the Eater.

Volume 2.3

As it relates to God and God and Man

Eternity happens to Himself in Himself and from the happening came creation per the Principles of His Consciousness, Himself. From He Who is the Beginning came the beginning of all things according to Himself and from Him Who is the End, and the End of all things according to Himself. Again, life must manifest in death and manifest as death, and this death is the consuming of life: Life consuming Itself in Itself from Itself by Itself. He is Life and the End of Life. He is Death Itself. His Life, Himself, is His Death: "No one takes my life. I lay it down." God consumed Himself. God consumes Himself. Further, we are all the Actual Possibilities of Eternity happening in Eternity according to Eternity. The end, what we reap, is Eternity Himself in manifestation, He is the manifestation of what we eat, the consequences within the parameters of Himself, the Cosmic Principle of Karma. To learn more about Death and God as Death read *Eternity Volume 4*.

Volume 3

Out of the Strong

Out of the strong: from the interiors of the strong. The inner chamber of the strong within the interiors of the strong. Now, strength produces strength and might produce might. Things produce themselves. The strong produce after themselves according to the Cosmic Principle of Imprint (Read Principle of Reality - Pillars That Constitute Reality Book 18 in Reality Series Volume 1 to gather more). And who is the strong one? The Lord Mighty in battle! From Him comes strength after strength. Might upon might. It is written: "The LORD your God in your midst, The Mighty One." Zephaniah 3:17 NKJV.

Volume 3.1

The Strong

"And to one he gave five talents, to another two, and to another one, to each according to his own ability…"
Mathew 25:15 NKJV

We are strong with differing strengths from the Strong One. We are all one reality diversely expressed in the might of the Mighty One that has apportioned Himself in His Might, Himself, to everyone according to their Might in the reality of the infinite multiple diversities of His Might, Himself. As it is written: "...each was given according to their ability." Ability is might, and this might is apportioned from the Mighty One and is a portion from His Infinite Might. The same portion apportioned from the Strong One is separate from the Strong though it came from the Strong One. It is Might from the Mighty One but not the Might of the Mighty One. Yet, it is a portion of the Mighty Ones Might. And what is this Might? The Spirit of Might, The Mighty Spirit, Eternity Himself. "What is stronger than a Lion?" That is, what is stronger than The Great Lion which is also, in another Kind of Itself from Itself, the Lion of Judah? The Lion of Judah is a Kind of the Spirit of Might and the Great

Lion is the Spirit of Might from Which has come the Lion of Judah. Eternity is the Eater!

Hierarchy of Might

"Now these were the heads of the mighty men whom David
had, who strengthened themselves with him in his
kingdom, with all Israel, to make him king, according to
the word of the LORD concerning Israel." 1 Chronicles
11:10 NKJV

"...high official watches over high official, and higher
officials are over them." Ecclesiastes 5:8 NKJV

Each according to his ability which is a portion from the
Mighty One, and a portion of the Mighty One made living
and given life. There are Higher Mighty Ones in the Mighty
One and Lower Mighty Ones in the Mighty One and all are
the Mighty One in His Infinite Hierarchy of Himself that is
Himself. Hence, the Great Lion and the Lion of Judah. The
former is greater than the latter. Yet, both are One Might, the
Mighty One and in His Might. Now, each one of us from the
Spirit of Might, as we all are, are certain portions of the
Mighty One according to the ranking of the Mighty One in
Himself. Some are a Higher Spirit of Might and others are a
Lesser Spirit of Might. Still, those that are embodiments and

portions of Higher Spirits of Might have other Higher Spirits of Might over them ad infinitum and those that are embodiments of Lesser Spirits of Might ad infinitum according to apportioning. There is a high for every high and a low for every low. A dimension within the dimension and a level within a level. A spirit and a spirit from spirit, spirits from spirit, and spirits from spirits from spirit within a spirit's structure of existence, which is Itself. This is the innate structure and manifestation of all consciousness from Itself through Itself by Itself according to its infinite multiple vast structure and reality, Itself. Every spirit, of men, angels, archangels, and other entities, including Eternity Himself, is variegated and is a variegated system of existence with lesser and higher versions of Itself in Itself. The Beginning point of the spirits and the endpoints of spirits. Note: Eternity has no beginning point and no end point, so His beginning point is non-existent and unsearchable. Ergo, the beginning point of His Power and Might, Himself, is Unsearchable in Power and Might. The least of Himself in Himself is least in appearance and structure within His contextualisation within the bounds of spirits and their becoming but is not least in potency though it is least in manifestation and becoming. Every God from God is as powerful as God is and is the power of God. Every spirit has spirits. You are a singular plurality. All spirits are singular pluralities.

Volume 3.1.2

Wisdom and Might

"The ants are a people not strong,

Yet they prepare their food in the summer..." Proverbs

30:25 NKJV

The wisdom of the mighty is their might and this might is mightier than the might of power. It is power greater than power; a power that defeats the strong in power. One strong in wisdom is stronger than one strong in power but weak in wisdom. Strength may win battles but wisdom wins wars and battles. A man weak in power is not weak in wisdom but a man strong in power may be weak in wisdom. And better than both is a man mighty in wisdom and mighty in power. The Lord is Wise, and the Lord is All-Powerful. He is Wisdom; He is Might.

Volume 3.2

Something Sweet

Now, the interiors and interior of the interiors of the strong and mighty are strength and might. The sweetness of might is victory. Victory comes from might. Victory is in might. And not merely in might but in the honour the mighty ones give the weak in the awareness of our oneness. We are strong for ourselves and strong for others. It is appointed for the strong to aid the weak and for the strong to aid themselves in their might. "Go in this might of yours..."Judges 6:14 NKJV. This means let your might be of benefit to you and to others. This is the sweetness, the pleasure, from the inner chamber of might. Victory for yourself and others is structured in your might. And victory for all is in the might of the Lord. The Mighty One became flesh and defeated Satan. Is He not the Spirit of Might? Out of the Strong, Jesus Christ, came Something Sweet, victory, and the pleasure of the Lord, Himself. The pleasure of might is might itself. The pleasure in might is in the wise administration of might in the same consciousness of might that is might itself.

Volume 3.3

Increasing in Might

When the strong have an understanding of power; from them comes sweetness, and that sweetness is power and victory in power with victory from power. The understanding of might is might to the mighty; might upon might making the mighty mightier. The knowledge of might is might to the mighty increasing their might in might. The wisdom of might is might upon might; might added to might, increasing the mighty in might. For there is power in understanding and understanding in power. Power in knowledge and knowledge in power. Wisdom in power and power in wisdom and might in understanding might. To increase in power understand power, know power, and gain the wisdom of power in power. Might is a Divine Intelligence in Whom resides In the Spirit of Might there is: wisdom of might, wisdom from might and wisdom in might with wisdom to might, knowledge of might, knowledge from might, and might of knowledge with knowledge to might, might of understanding and understanding in might with understanding of might and understanding to might, fear of might, fear from might and fear in might with fear to might.

Unless the man of might operates from the above in the Spirit of Might, he shall perish. Did Samson not perish in his might? Even the mighty perish in their might. In gathering these we scale the dimensions and levels of Might. And what are these but Spirits of the Spirit of Might, Spirits of Might from the Spirit of Might in the Spirit of Might? Still, the understanding of power generates counsel in the power. The counsel of power. A man that understands might possess the counsel of might. The same comes to this by knowledge of might in understanding might whence from comes wisdom of might and wisdom in might.

Self-Control

It takes might to govern the self and that might is Itself. The self is power and is with power. The power of self must apply to self being Itself which applies itself to Itself, from Itself, by Itself in Itself and through Itself because the self is a self-interacting reality. The self applies its power to Itself in Its might, Itself. This is self-control - a dimension of might, a spirit of might - a Divine Spirit - the Spirit of Might. The same is governing might - the power to govern. Power controls power. Every power carries the potency to control itself because every power is a principle to itself. Still, it takes power to subdue power and power to increase power. Again, it takes power to govern power; a higher power governs a high power that governs over a lower power that is a higher power in the order of power and powers in power. A power devoid of governance comes to ruin.

"Whoever has no rule over his own spirit
Is like a city broken down, without walls. "Proverbs 25:28
NKJV

Volume 3.4

The Perishing of the Mighty Ones

"A wise man scales the city of the mighty,
And brings down the trusted stronghold." Proverbs 21:22
NKJV

When the mighty lack knowledge of their might they perish. When the mighty lack knowledge in their might they perish. Still, when the mighty lack knowledge of themselves they perish. The same perish when they lack growth in their might and of their might in the knowledge of their might by understanding their might and becoming wise in might by the wisdom of might in might's wisdom. For the governance of might is in might's wisdom, knowledge, understanding, and reverence. When the mighty lack these of that which they have; they perish. Even the mighty perish. Did not Samson perish in His might and in the Lord's Might because of lack of knowledge? Yet, did he not show himself to be with knowledge and of knowledge, and wise in knowledge by might's wisdom and knowledge by giving a riddle? The same knew the covenant behind his power and articulated it to Delilah. Even the mighty perish in their might. By the wisdom of the Philistines, the strongman was defeated. Lack of wisdom causes the mighty to perish, the wise man strong in wisdom binds the strongman, strong in power, and rules over him. By wisdom the wise rule over the strong. By wisdom the wise rule over the mighty. Might makes a warrior but wisdom makes a wise warrior and a wise ruler. A man with might and wisdom becomes a wise warrior and a wise ruler.

Out of The Eater

"Then God said, "Let the earth bring forth the living creature according to its kind: cattle and creeping thing and beast of the earth, each according to its kind"; and it was so." Genesis 1:24 NKJV

The eater was a Lion that belongs to the physical system. An emergence from the physical system, and is the representation of the physical system. Therefore, out of the eater means out of the inner principles of the physical system that determine the operations of the physical system. The physical system is an eater! An eating system that will consume and devour you from its inner reality and workings. Eaters are barely discerned by their physical reality. It takes discernment, seeing into the physical, to see and know the eaters in and of the physical system. These are men and women that embody wicked diverse spirits, agents of darkness, poverty, anger, rage, lovers of money, and people of hate. Men operating in the aforementioned ruin themselves and others. They are believers found in churches, pigs that shouldn't receive petals lest they trampled on them and turn around to devour you. Religious men in priestly authority, and men of authority on diverse dimensions in the physical system from the government to the church. Isn't the Lion the Long of the Jungle? These eaters are men and women of authority serving in diverse regions and places including the home.

Volume 4.1

The Enemy

"So Samson went down to Timnah with his father and mother, and came to the vineyards of Timnah. Now *to his* surprise, a young lion *came* roaring against him." Judges 14:5 NKJV

Whatever comes against you, that is your enemy. The eater, the Lion, was an enemy of Samson. Your enemies in the spiritual realm and physical system are eaters. Devourers that seek to consume you. Some make themselves your enemies, others are made into your enemies through manipulation, hate, selfishness, comparison, jealousy, bitterness, and unforgiveness. Again, the eater represents the intelligence and Cosmic Principle of Opposition, which, the enemy of mankind and his devils embody. Satan means enemy. Still, you are included as an eater that can eat yourself! Consciousness is a Principle of Consciousness. You are your greatest enemy, Satan. You are your own opposition hence the need for self-control, which is the intelligence and consciousness of winning the battle against yourself which is yourself. Consciousness is the Cosmic Principle of Opposition as an authority to Itself. There are many eaters, and enemies, but every person is an enemy to themselves. You make yourself what you are. Out of the eater means out of you. Out of yourself comes your enemy, yourself, in the reality of yourself (proclivities and inclinations). Now, inclinations are according to types: self-generated, inherited, affiliate and or associative. The consciousness you inherit can be an enemy, in which case the forefathers and parents become enemies, the eater, of their generations. Associative propensities are based on friendships and marriage. There is what you become by virtue of relationship (relationship is for becoming). It is written: "Bad company ruins good morals." Friends that corrupt you and cause you to compromise and loose yourself are eaters of destiny and yourself. Whatever rules over you and hinders your progress is your eater. Whatever corrupts good morals is an enemy of the good. Whoever corrupts your good morals, is your enemy.

Came Something to Eat

The food came out of the eater. That is, out of the physical system, and out of the enemies of man that include man. Verily, Earth is the physical system from which the food of man comes. Food is part of the physical system, cones from within the physical system. It is stated: "Let the Earth produce every tree according to its kind...and herbs." Again, "I have given you these for food." Out of the physical system comes bread. So, "man shall not live by bread alone..." This means man shall not live by the physical system: the Cosmic Principle of Seed and Fruit with the Cosmic Principles of Increase and Multiplication. The same operates via work. The seed must be planted to produce fruit and seed. Multiplication and increase are by work. " Man shall not live by bread alone..." That is, man shall not live by the physical system. The same is: man shall not eat according to the physical system alone "...but by every word that comes out of the mouth of the Lord." That is, by the Eternal System that eats from Itself and on Itself. Eternity is His system of living. Man shall live by the Eternal System, Eternity Himself. He shall eat from Himself, from the God within and survive by the God within, Which is the word from the mouth of Lord, Himself. Verily, the physical system is sustained by the same. Living by bread is a dimension of living from the word, a working of the word, and not by the word. To live by the word is to transcend the physical system of eating bread and come to living by every Word, the Cosmic Food that is Eternity in His Infinite Multiple Diverse Expansions and Expressions of Himself as bread: "...the Bread that came down from heaven, "...the Word became flesh." That is, the word became the physical system. The flesh is the physical system that eats Itself to survive. Ergo, man is an eater of the physical system. You are an eater of the physical system; of seed and fruit, the produce of the Earth, the physical system.

Spoils

"But when a stronger than he comes upon him and overcomes him, he takes from him all his armour in which he trusted, and divides his spoils." Luke 11:12 NKJV

When the enemy is defeated, spoil is taken. Plunder is taken from the enemy and this can be something to eat or something to use to get something to eat, monies and or property that can be sold and used to get something to eat. There are enemies that carry something to eat. Defeating them is accessing food. There are battles whose victory is bread; according to the spiritual system and physical system. Didn't the lepers get food from their enemies? "And when these lepers came to the outskirts of the camp, they went into one tent and ate and drank, and carried from it silver and gold and clothing, and went and hid *them;* then they came back and entered another tent, and carried *some* from there *also,* and went and hid *it.* " 2 Kings 7:8 NKJV Out of them came something to eat. Food, spiritual and physical, is part of the spoil of warriors engaged in battle.

Volume 4.2.1.2

Eating from the Eater

That which eats you can feed you. The eater feeds when subdued: "Out of the eater something to eat. "Out of" means from that which the eater owns. Everything has something in it. Every eater has something to be eaten.

Chapter 2

Samson

"So the woman bore a son and called his name Samson,
and the child grew, and the Lord blessed him." Judges
13:24 NKJV

Beyond being a Nazarite, Samson was an embodiment of the Spirit of Might, of the Great Lion and Eater, Eternity Himself; the Devourer of the devourers, the Eater of eaters: "I will devour the devourer for you." He was a kind of Spirit of Might, a kind of Lion from the Great Lion. He had been apportioned the Spirit of Might and with it the knowledge of might, the wisdom of might, and the understanding of might with the counsel of might. It is from these that he articulates and creates the riddle which demonstrates and communicates the wisdom, understanding, and knowledge of God conjoined to his understanding of the Spirit of Might. It is written: "The words of the wise and their riddles. " Proverbs 1.6 NKJV. The words of the wise and their riddles! Samson was wise in power. He was wise by the Spirit of Might in Whom resides the Spirit of Wisdom He did not speak from himself but from the understanding of the Mighty One and from the Mighty One. By the understanding of might, in the knowledge of might, with the wisdom of might did Samson judge Israel. In the Wisdom of the Spirit of Might, and in the Wisdom in the Spirit of Might, with the Knowledge of the Spirit of Might, in the Knowledge of the Spirit of Might, and in the Understanding of the Spirit of Might, with the Spirit of Understanding did Samson judge Israel.

The Prophecy of Samson to Samson

From Samson the eater of the Philistines came something to eat; And out of the strong, Samson, came something sweet. Delilah bought food that was sweet to the stomach through the money. Again, the money afforded her other pleasures such as clothes and as many as are such pleasures. In that riddle, Samson prophesied to Himself by the Spirit of the Lord. The Riddle is a Prophesy to Samson by Samson. The Spirit of Might in Him knew His end and by His Counsel and Wisdom spoke to Samson in his riddle to others. The knowledge of might in the Spirit of Might knows all things.

"Now the lords of the Philistines gathered together to offer a great sacrifice to Dagon their god, and to rejoice. And they said: "Our god has delivered into our hands Samson our enemy!" Judges 16:23 NKJV

The Prophecy of Samson on the Coming Messiah

Out of the Eater, Jesus Christ - the Lion of Judah, came something to eat, Himself. "Unless you eat my flesh and drink my blood you shall not have eternal life." He is humanity's divine food. The food of His divinity. The food of man's divinity is Eternity. The same, as proved earlier is the Mighty One, the Great Lion from Whom came something sweet, victory and life in abundance. "In His right arm are pleasures forever more." In the same riddle, Samson spoke and gave a prophecy concerning a stronger and mightier Lion greater than himself that would come, the Lion of and the pleasures that would come forth from him to those born of Him from Him. He prophesied of the coming of the Messiah. Again, Out of the Eater, the Great Lion came something to Eat, the Lion of Judah, Jesus the Christ: "I am the living bread which came down from heaven." John 6:51 NKJV. The Lion of Judah is the something to eat out of the Eater and is the Eater in an Expansion of Himself from Himself. Still, out of the Strong, which is stronger than the Lion, the Eater came something sweet, victory and life abundant. And the Divine Honey, the Lion Himself. The same, something sweet, is the wine of the New Covenant, the blood of Christ which is in the Eater, Christ (blood is in the body): "Unless you eat the flesh of the Son of Man, and drink His blood you have no life in you." John 6:53 NKJV

Samson, Philistine, and Israel

Out of the Eater, Samson - the eater of the Philistines, came something to eat for Israel. Again, out of the strong, Samson, came something sweet, victory, and hope for Israel. Still, what is stronger than a Lion? Samson, who killed the Lion. And what is sweeter than honey? Freedom. On the same: every food is sweeter in freedom. What is sweet is made sweeter by freedom. Oppression deprives sweetness of that which is sweet; though it is sweet, its sweetness is limited by chains. Out the eater came something to eat: from the eater of Philistine, Samson, came food from the oppression of the Philistines on the Israelites. Further, out of the strong came something sweet to the Philistines, the joy and happiness of capturing Samson.

Volume 4

The Eater of Samson

The eater can eat himself by failing to discipline himself, by pride, anger, hate, and sexual immorality. Samson the eater ate himself by trusting Delilah, who was another eater of Samson. She contributed to his ruin and delivered him to the Philistines who devoured his sight. By eating himself, Samson was eaten. Nothing can ruin man other than that which is in man, and that which becomes in man becoming the man.

"When Delilah saw that he had told her all his heart, she sent and called for the lords of the Philistines, saying, "Come up once more, for he has told me all his heart." So the lords of the Philistines came up to her and brought the money in their hand. Then she lulled him to sleep on her knees, and called for a man and had him shave off the seven locks of his head. Then she began to torment him, and his strength left him." Judges 16:18-19 NKJV

Something to Eat and Something Sweet for Samson

His might was of benefit to him. It was sweet to Him: "Out of the strong something sweet." The might of the mighty is sweet to the mighty. Power is sweet to him that has it and sweeter to him that commands it. Not all that have power possess the intelligence to command power. And by that, they are short of might in their might and lack might in their might. All mighty men are diverse in might.

Chapter 4

The Seven Spirits - The Eaters

"Out of the eater something to eat; And out of the strong something sweet." Judges 14:14 NKJV

It has been proved that the Lord is the Eater. He is the Eater of the eaters. The Great Lion, the Devourer of all things, and of all devourers. Now, in Him rests something to eat, and out of Him came something to eat, Jesus the Christ - the Bread from Heaven, Eternity Himself; in Whom rests and resides the Seven Spirits. And what is Christ? A Kind of Eater from the Eater. He is the Lion of Judah! That is, the Eater of Judah, Which are the Seven Spirits. He is the Embodiment of the Seven Spirits. He is the Seven Spirits in flesh. The Seven Spirits are the Devourers and respectively, each is a Devourer. Remember: Samson was the eater of the Philistine, He was a Kind of Eater from the Spirit of Might, Which is a Kind of Eater. Samson is a Kind within a Kind; that is, he is a kind from a Kind; a kind of Lion from a Kind of Lion that is not the Lion of Judah, which is greater than the Lion that Samson is and was. Samson originated from the Spirit of Might. The spirit soul known as Samson is from the realm of might. The mighty men of David are also from

50

this realm of Eternity. They, and Samson, are made in the image and likeness of the Spirit of Might.

The Hiding Place

The Lord is hidden in Himself, as seen in the first chapter. The Seven Spirits are the Lord, and these are Hidden in Themselves and Each is hidden in the other as a Lesser Spirit of the Other. Each of the Seven Lions is in the Seven Lions. The Devourer's hiding Place is the Devourer.

Volume 1.1

The Spirit of Wisdom

Wisdom is mighty in Her might, which is Spirit, the Spirit of Might. She is with knowledge of her wisdom in the knowledge of her knowledge and is with knowledge in her wisdom, the Spirit of Knowledge, Which begins in the fear of the Lord, the Spirit of the Fear of the Lord. Again, by Her knowledge and wisdom comes counsel that is in Her as Her. Counsel rests on the wise, the Spirit of Counsel, which comes by the Spirit of the Lord and is in the Spirit of the Lord Which is the Holy Spirit by Which the Word, became flesh: the Seven Spirit became flesh; and this by the Power of the Holy Spirit; that is, by the Spirit of Power/Might Which is the Spirit of the Lord. The same was done by the Counsel of the Seven Spirit, Which is the Council of the Lord and is the Spirit of the Lord. And what is the Spirit of Knowledge? She is the Spirit of the Lord.

The Spirit of the Fear of the Lord

The fear of the Lord is the beginning of knowledge. That is; the Spirit of the Fear of the Lord is the beginning of the Spirit of Knowledge. Again, the fear of the Lord is the beginning of wisdom; the Spirit of the Fear of the Lord is the beginning of Wisdom: "The fear of the Lord is the beginning of wisdom..." Proverbs 9:10 NKJV. Again, it is written: "...the knowledge of the Holy One is understanding." Proverbs 9:10 NKJV. The same is: the Spirit of Knowledge, begins in the Spirit of the Fear of the Lord, and is the Spirit of Understanding, the Holy One. That is, in the knowledge of the Holy One by the Spirit of Knowledge in the Spirit of the Fear of the Lord, Which is the Spirit of the Lord, comes the understanding of the Holy One, that is the Spirit of Understanding, Which is the Spirit of the Lord. Still, the Spirit of the Lord is Mighty, the Spirit of the Fear of the Lord is Mighty - is the Spirit of Might in the Fear of the Lord, Itself. It is the Spirit of the Lord, mighty in His Might and wise in the wisdom of might, the Spirit of Might. Again, the Fear of the Lord is the beginning of knowledge, of the Spirit of Knowledge Which is mighty in knowledge - the Spirit of

Might, wise in Knowledge, the Spirit of Wisdom - where counsel resides, the Spirit of Counsel.

Volume 1.3

The Spirit of Knowledge

The Spirit of Knowledge begins in the Spirit of the Fear of the LORD, Which is the Spirit of the LORD. In Knowledge resides the might of Knowledge, the Spirit of Might, in the Same resides the wisdom of Knowledge and the wisdom in knowledge - the Spirit of Wisdom, and the counsel of Knowledge and the counsel in Knowledge, the Spirit of Counsel. Again, the aforementioned comes with the understanding of knowledge, the understanding of the wisdom of knowledge in knowledge, the understanding of counsel, and the understanding in counsel, and that of fear - the Spirit of Understanding.

The Spirit of Counsel

Counsel is given from understanding, the Spirit of Understanding, the same is given from a knowing, the Spirit of Knowledge, to understand is to know and unless you know you cannot give counsel. Again, in the Spirit of Counsel resides the knowledge of counsel, the wisdom of counsel - the Spirit of Wisdom, the fear of counsel, the Spirit of the Fear of the LORD, and the understanding of counsel, the Spirit of Understanding. Still, the Spirit of Counsel is the Spirit of the LORD wherein resides the Might of the LORD that is Himself, the Spirit of Might; the Might of Counsel and in Counsel.

Volume 1.5

The Spirit of Might

Samson was in the image and likeness of the Spirit of Might and from this He demonstrated understanding, knowledge, wisdom, and counsel. Did he not rule over Israel? Was he not a judge? In his ruling he made judgements and, in his judgements, there was counsel, the Spirit of Counsel, from the Spirit of Might. Again, doesn't the LORD call Samson wise? Proverbs 1:6. Samson was wisdom hidden in might, the Spirit of Wisdom, in the Spirit of Might. Did he not give a riddle with words of understanding? He is the Spirit of Understanding hidden in the Spirit of Might. He ruled and gave counsel to Israel. He is the Spirit of Counsel Hidden in the Spirit of Might. Counsel is given in the understanding of knowledge. He is the Spirit of Knowledge hidden in the Spirit of Might. Further, the Spirit of Knowledge begins in the Spirit of the Fear of the LORD, He is the Spirit of the Fear of the LORD hidden in the Spirit of Might. Again, the fear of the Lord is the beginning of wisdom; that is, the Spirit of the Fear of the LORD is the beginning of the Spirit of Wisdom.

Volume 1.6

The Spirit of Understanding

To know is to understand and to understand is to know to understand: the Knowledge of the Holy One is Understanding. That is, the Spirit of Knowledge is the Spirit of Understanding. Ergo, the Spirit of Understanding is the Spirit of Knowledge: to know is to understand and to understand is to know. Now, in knowing understanding, one knows knowledge, and in knowing knowledge one knows understanding and to understand knowledge in understanding is wisdom, the Spirit of Wisdom. Again, to understand knowledge is to have counsel in knowledge, the Spirit of Counsel. Still, understanding is a might, it is a power, and strength of the mind, the Spirit of Might, Which is the Spirit of the LORD, the Same is the Spirit of the Fear of the LORD.

Volume 1.7

The Spirit of the LORD

The Spirit of the LORD is the LORD, and all that He is the Spirit is. And This Spirit is the Holy Spirit, an Expansion of Eternity from Eternity. The fullness of God from God: His Might, His Wisdom, His Knowledge, His Understanding, His Reverence and Awe, the Fear of the LORD, Which is Himself. The Seven Spirits are the Holy Spirit, Emanations, and Expansions from the Holy Spirit. They are in Him and are Him from Himself, Who is the LORD from the LORD.

Seven Subtleties of the Seven Spirits

"To understand a proverb and an enigma,

The words of the wise and their riddles." Proverbs 1:6

NKJV

The riddles of the wise (Spirit of Wisdom) are given in words of understanding (the Spirit of Understanding) that conceal knowledge (the Spirit of Knowledge) by their counsel (Spirit of Counsel) in the might of their knowledge wisdom, and understanding (Spirit of Might); for in their wisdom and knowledge, they revere and stand in awe (the Spirit of the Fear of the Lord) of the ways of wisdom in her knowledge and understand through her might and spirit which is by the Spirit of the Lord. The Seven Spirits are Subtle in their wisdom and understanding hiding Themselves in their expressions and words using their Might. It is the pleasure of the Lord, Who is Spirit and is His Own Spirit, to hide a matter by His Seven Spirits and in His Seven Spirits. The riddle is the Seven Spirits concealed and revealed by One Spirit of the Seven Spirits Which is the Spirit of the Lord. There are, therefore, Seven Subtilties of the Seven Spirits, that are the Seven Spirits in the riddle. Are

the Seven not Seven Devourers that are The One Devourer?
It is written: "...the Lion (Devourer) of the tribe of Judah."
Revelations 5:5 NKJV. the Seven are hidden in the riddle
and revealed by the same in the same.

"It is the glory of God to conceal a matter,
But the glory of kings *is* to search out a matter." Proverbs
25:2 NKJV

Volume 2.1

The Seven Teachers

"To understand a proverb and an enigma,

The words of the wise and their riddles." Proverbs 1:6

NKJV

Words of understanding are words of wisdom from the counsel of wisdom in the understanding of knowledge by the might of the wise, who are spirits, from the Spirit of the LORD, and are portions of the Spirit of the LORD from the Same. And these, the wise, stand in awe of wisdom. Therefore, by means of their words, they teach the means of their words and their structure, the aforementioned that are the Seven Spirits of the LORD that are lord Himself. Each of the Seven Spirits teaches about each of the Seven Spirits and in their operations, and undertakings, the Seven operate from the Seven in each. The riddle of Samson is the Seven Spirits concealed and expressed. Out of the wisdom of might, in the knowledge of might in might, and the counsel of might with the awe and fear of might in might with the understanding of might in might by the Spirit of the LORD did Samson construct the riddle. The riddle is the work of Seven Spirits in and by the Seven Spirits.

Chapter 5

Something Sweet, Sweeter than Honey

"What is sweeter than honey? And what is stronger than a lion?" Judges 14:18 NKJV

Out of the Eater something to eat, and this is the LORD Himself, as seen thus far, Which is the Seven Spirits, Jesus the Christ, Who is the Word. They asked Samson questions in response to his riddle because they had received the answer in plan form from his bride-to-be. It was not merely a response from men but a response from the Lord through men.

The First: What is stronger than a Lion? The answer is the LORD. The Great Lion, the Lion of Judah.

The Second: What is sweeter than honey? The Lord. It is written: "How sweet are Your words to my taste, Sweeter than honey to my mouth!" Psalm 119:103 NKJV. A man is his words. The LORD is His words! He is sweeter than honey. The Lord, the Something to Eat from the Eater is sweeter than honey. His words are Him, and He is the Seven

Spirits. His words are the Seven Spirit and are with the Seven Spirits. Again, it is written: "Oh, taste and see that the Lord is good; Blessed is the man who trusts in Him!" Psalm 34:8 NKJV. That which is good is sweet and this is the Lord, Who is sweeter than honey: "How sweet are Your words to my taste, Sweeter than honey to my mouth!" Psalm 119:103 NKJV

Chapter 6

Something to Eat that Eats

"The sweetest honey is loathsome in its own deliciousness. And in the taste destroys the appetite." William Shakespeare, Romeo and Juliet

Out of the eater something to eat. That is, out of the inner structure of the Eater comes something to eat. This means that something to eat has the potency to eat. The food from the eater is the eater. That which you eat has the potency to eat you: "The sweetest honey…destroys appetite." William Shakespeare. It is written: "It is not good to eat much honey..." Proverbs 25:27 NKJV. The sweetness that overcomes you and takes charge of you eats you. Aren't there men and women enslaved to good things? Food, sex, and such as the creations of good which are good. Be careful not to be eaten by what you eat. Everything you eat is an eater with the potency to eat you.

Out of the Strong Something Sweet

Praise is sweet to the strong. The praise of the strong comes from their strength. Therefore, the sweet is strong because it is out of the strong. It is as strong as the strength it has come from. Is the Lord not praised for His Strength? Praise is sweet to the Lord. Again, praise emerging from the strength of the Lord, on account of the display of His strength, is strength to the one that praises His strength. But it is not good to seek one's own glory: "It is not good to eat much honey; So to seek one's own glory is not glory." Proverbs 25:27 NKJV. Wasn't King Saul defeated by the sweetness of praise on account of his might apportioned him from the Lord? The praise he received was not enough for him though it was enough according to the measure of might accorded and apportioned to him by God. He wanted more than what was his portion and in pursuit of more, of more sweetness from his strength, he was beaten and defeated by his own pursuit. The sweetness of power is according to power; this returns to the power with the same dose of power. The same can overcome the man (generic). By his measure of power, from the Powerful One, was King Saul overtaken.

"So the women sang as they danced, and said:

"Saul has slain his thousands,

And David his ten thousands."

Then Saul was very angry, and the saying displeased him; and he said, "They have ascribed to David ten thousands, and to me they have ascribed *only* thousands. Now *what* more can he have but the kingdom?" 1 Samuel 18:7-8 NKJV